Under the Mermaid Moon

Fluctisonant Press

Under the Mermaid Moon

John Henry Rolston

Fluctisonant Press

The Doctor of our souls has placed the
remedy in the hidden regions of the soul
- St. John Cassian

A seeker went to ask a sage for guidance
on the Sufi way. The Sage counseled:
"If you have never trodden the path of love,
go away, fall in love, then come back to us"
- Nur ad-Din Abd ar-Rahman Jami

<u>Poems</u>

When you get here
And you get to the train tracks
There's parking
You need to take a path along
The tracks
When you get here

Some people live colorful lives
But mine is but black on white
Some are filled with all kinds of spice
I'm happy to live line by line

Some clouds roam from town to town
Celebrating with music much too loud
Some oceans carouse wild and bestial
So even old Neptune spirits with sprites

But let me be a long dried riverbed
With crusty old rocks for friends
And I would treasure each of each day
Whittling words far from the conurbation

What cemetery holds
    The dead angels
Who fought and were slain
By the sword of Gabriel

I would like to slip in
    One night
And steal away with
    Their silvery wings
Now that they haven't need

Maybe with some tinkering
    With their engineering
I could get by with
    Masquerading
And cryptically
    Entertain
        A gypsy

Do I have to worry
Without hurry
Casually humiliated
Suspiciously religiously
Debilitated
And just like a conspiracy
Secretly, so to solicit
Justification
Becomes even more embarrassing
Barbarically insipidly
And in the end
Weakening and willowy
Wearily
And without a hurry
Crushingly and without anger
Angrily

I have no more love to give
It's all been spent
Or is locked up
      In a chest
      Without a key
In the temple of Solomon
Draped over a covenant
         Sometimes visible in battle

I have no more life to give
It's all been strewn across the grassy days
Gone, lodged between the stones
      Wedged and
      Rusted
And built upon by some Babylon
To be lost some day
      Maybe within the sea

I have no more dreams to winter with
No more hopes to hope with
I have no more interest in the clouds
      Just a moon to wonder at
      With knowledge of the past
And a shroud with bloody imprints
To guess and reason with debate
      And incense

Why does the winter wait so long
The hooded sky linger gracelessly
Not that I am complaining
But I can't be sure

The laughing Buddha seems to frown at me
And dancing Shiva stands and stares
And I think I saw Narayana walking away
But I can't be sure

I spent my whole life searching
For something never found
And though I failed
The rain feels like sun

Discovering something doesn't exist
Like the proof of arithmetic
Funny, though I know it is futile,
Yet we persist

A bee can pester from flower to flower
But return without pollen
A spacecraft can travel forever and ever
And yet we and they will never know for certain

Why does the summer sulk so long
Blue skies longing to turn brown
Not that I am complaining
Pretending to know for sure

19

I'd like to know where the end is
So I'd know where to begin
Backward from there and forward
      Simultaneously
That's the only possible way
To know whether to remember
      Or forget
I once heard that in the game of chess
The endgame begins with
The first pawns advance
And even some have said
The game is over when
      It hasn't even begun
Some have walked out shaking
Their sullen heads saying
Even some hell deserving monster
From their deathbed is heaven fit

      Didn't Jesus kiss the stunned Judas
      And congratulate Barabbas

The surface can only be known
By the depths
As some fish are best in
Desert quest
I have found sometimes
What I had never lost
And never sought for what
I have sought
A checkmated king raises its
Arms in victory; and
As heaven keeps open its gates
For the reprobate
I have stood wondering
      Like a hobo in a steel ferry
      Across rivers of land
In wonderment at this mystery
And whether I should take the step

I could stare at your legs every day
Whether in parade or lying still
In the distance or close to carressness

I could glare, when you are not looking,
Though you may sense my idolatry
So I must glance away despairingly occasionally

Your arms my cupidity, your neck my cacoëthes
Your eyes demonize my thoughts and wouldbe actions
Your breasts the impulsor of my lecherousness

But the manifest of your legs nearby
And my libidinousness is catered to unopposed
And my erotomaniac heart wanders in dream

Until even I stare and glare at myself disapprovingly
Repulsed at its illegalityness

21   Don't be a flower
Grateful for the bee
    Any bee
Canonizing each moon
While deifying the sun
Straining the stalk to see each ray
    Any ray
Demonizing the soil
Thanking the sky for
Each drop of rain
    Every drop
Criticizing each and every bug
That happens near
Whether landing on your petal
    Or not
Stretching taller and taller
Until you stop
Then drooping lower and lower
    And lower
Finally in the end
Wondering if the sun
Which sometimes was and
    Sometimes weren't
Was worth being a flower
And not a worm

I love a dress that
      Is undressed quickly with
          Just a nudge
Whether done privately for
      Personal depravity
Or purposely accidentally
        Publicly
        Simplistically
But obviously
      Maybe a bit too perversely
But enjoyably embarrassing
If only momentarily
      Or more, daringly
I could be close at hand
      Or further
        Bodyguard or spectator
Planned unplanned
      With or without a fan
But only once only
      Or twice
        Maybe thrice
Such for me is perfect
        Heaven, my heaven

If roses are rong
Then no one is wright
My heart, waning gibbous,
Declares
Pure days in platonic prayer
To prepare for
Celled nights knotted in not
I dare naughty thoughts
Their worse
Invitingly
Vases void of stems, though
Tables strewn with petals
 Though crinkled, like thoughts
I work all day in the garden
Leaning on the rake
Afraid

My heaven, yes, contains hell
While the rest of earth is just earth
I crave what destroys me
Quickly as slowly as possible
Until the far off end is even farther

With skies full of deceitful sparrows
And oceans full of fish that falsify
The mountains have bushes that burn
        But not with wisdom
And I believe that I have been tricked:
The fairy tales are fairyless

My heaven hath a heavenly hell
But better than a heaven that is heavenless
Streams have a rocky bottom
Oceans deadly currents
So my heart is shaped so

Born to grow and shrink and die
Monkish horrors to moralless delights
Love gets to love
        Through loveless quest
And heaven is hell in the end
Given mermaids cannot walk the land

25

I have a lOΘve that
I must hide, not of bΘΘks
(Or at least most) my thΘΘugths
Can be fΘΘund bΘΘund to
This tΘΘ desired, inspired
CΘΘntemplated almΘΘst heaven
Until nΘΘthing else is left
To inspire tΘΘ except this (these)(shes)
My mind is left pΘΘleased
In dreΘΘam
Of mermaids ΘΘ

If it wasn't for John
Dillinger I'd
Probably been a saint
Fat Tony made me
Want to add to my
Plate
But Nelson with his
Baby face really
Clinched the deal

I could have been
Laid in my grave
With a Republican
Pin upon my lapel
But Pretty Boy Floyd
Was just the guy
To teach me how to
Sin

So instead of a holy
Card, a mug shot
Displays my image
And all I have is a
Rose to hold to remind
Me of what could have
Been

Sitting on a rock resting
While on the road from Damascus
I witnessed the most extraordinary sight
Which none would believe
Even my priest
Even me
While pounding the table in the most
Ridiculous way I'm afraid I forget what I say
But no matter – no one is there to hear
Or to remember the display
Powerful waves tear and crumble
Mountains hurl with the most terrible attacks
It is like the storm which washes the roads
So nobody knows the crimes that it knows
Beautiful stars disguise the chaotic disgrace of space
But from my rock
I saw his face and his fear made me afraid
So I ran away

Such a puzzle this
She has the prayers I wish I could pray
She has the smile I wish I could smile
She has the heart I wish I had but can't

I know how to wander deserts
I know how to weather weather
I know all the paths that are not paths
But she has the heart I wish I had but can't
Such a puzzle this

I am a puzzle but with a missing piece
I am a rainfall with one drop out of place
An ocean which scours the shore but with a missing wave
I'm traveling all the way on the Pacific train
But I missed a stop

She has the hand I hold though I don't
She has the lips I kiss if I could kiss
And the breasts I keep abreast in the wind
No puzzle this – just a wish
A wish that can't be wished that's wished

Can you help me find the kiss
That I so so missed
Like a butterfly it flit nearby
Flit so close but on approach
It flit far
As waves curled and crashed
Beneath the assenting moon
Only to recede before touching toes
As clouds craved to caress clouds
My lips craved to caress lips
To linger as the wind lingers
Among the leaves while crawling
Between the trees fingering every limb
Finding hidden things
Hidden things dared to find
Dare I caress as the rising tide
Caresses the sloping naked shoreline
Rising to lap before the hidden
Cave
Will you soon allow me linger
Upon your lips and wander
About the bowers in search of flowers
Like an ocean of wind upon the land

Did you hear that? That
Was my death
Cornice dreams
Theanlage of hate
Purulent thoughts
Carbonundum squeals
Exigenct desires
Mutated fears, hayden soul
Kayoodling
The skirl of joys
Drowned out by the
Silence of death

I heard it
And it haunts me
To this day

Do tadpoles know frogs
      And caterpillars butterflies
Is it difficult for birds
      To know a peach is coming
Not all lightening
      Impregnates earth
But I hope they all were
      Born with hope
I know sinners damned
      To hell still hold out
      Hope of Trappist prayers
So shouldn't I
Who has memorized
Her smile

It doesn't matter to me
I have left so many novels
      Unfinished
Abandoned so many stories
      Even before writ
Why should this be
      Any different
Doesn't magic always
Have its dulling explanations
Summers cool rain its
      Aftermath of humidity
Even the promise of a
Forgiving heaven its
      Eventual reality
Remember self that
Winter was not so worse
Before the spring

And in the brownish night
Under the spying moon
So many invisible messengers
      Flitting about
Into the evening
      Morning looms

And with it
    Another hand unheld
Dismember your vacant
Web my friend
While considering the moth
And a thousand possibilities
Then construct another
Fortifying yourself
Against the perpetual
Inevitability

One more flight, my
Friendly owl not
Especially fooling yourself
One more gurgle pretending
A giggle before you
Go my companion frog
Another night maybe
    Brown maybe red
Shall doubtless wend
Another moon yet to spy upon
As it reflects

I don't believe in god; why should I
Self-exiled in this forgotten monastery
       Harboring in a dusty cell
Laboring in a forgotten dusty garden
           While kneeling all the while
Glad and fearful of the bell for supper
Flagellation as dessert after cabbage soup
Between sub tuum and akathist
Before plankish rest and dark cold

Angels though know – now that is is more is –
Ladies dressed and undressed in white with wings
Hovering near and sometimes whispering in my ear
Mermaids dancing in the waves
       Beckoning me to join the spray
Fairies, my consiglieres, answering my prayers
With playful quodlibets and sparkling smiles
Pan Jin Lian, Bes and Lofn – the deities which waken me
While I wait for Mami Wata to abduct me tantivy to eternity

The desert lays twice a desert
After the defalcation
And heat feels twice the heat
And thirst is thrice thirst

Clearly, the monk has learned,
Fasting is easier without the crust of bread
And bears kneel because they know
Winter is worse with less snow

Talk to the bee of the field of flowers
Watch the fish when it's worse with water
And many a man has hung himself
When his billions have been cut in half

And yet
Persecutors learned that less torture is torturous
Heaven withholds holiness for faithful followers
A widow knows a mite is a mite too much
And yet the esurient heart remains untaught

I took a step past salvation
The shank of the other side really
And I really wasn't really going to stay
Realizing my mistake
Arriving where I didn't belong
But then I later learned
Was a pirate's fairy
Bid me stay
Still I know
Because the still blue water
Wasn't still and wasn't blue
And even wasn't even water
But it wasn't the pirates'
Fairy's bidding that made
Me stay
I'd heard many a fairies
Bidding before and knew
It was usually a mistake
To heed the bidding

One step past salvation
One step too many was a step enough
One step reeling to escape
One step in was a hundred back

A lifetime past salvation is barely a day
And I lived it mostly walking
Not directly to escape
But also ignoring fairies and roses
Favored by beloved bees
       Chosen then forgotten
And followed by variegated butterflies
Fair-haired and white headed
They seemed lost but directed
With lycanthropic distraction
Twice I needed to rest and once
Beside a lake in the greenery
Hidden from all but the snakes and spiders
Really to rest from bewildering

To simply stare at the startled moon
And then once in the greenery beside a lake
To shelter from the stare of the staring moon
Because there was nowhere else to go
Though but one step from salvation

I am nothing
        If not nobody
A leaf even a breeze
        Would not breeze
An asteroid you may notice
        Passing unnoticed
Quietly in sanctuary
With mermaid dreams
        Apounding me

I could never be
        In the darkness
Like a firefly
        For all to see
Or the lone flag on
        A solitary pole
For show and saluted
As if something more
        Than dirty fabric

I am just a rusted Pontiac
Hidden in some lost mountains crevice
Overgrown by some
        Invasive plant
A fabricated monk in a
        Fabricated shack

As I sit enjoying the sunshine
Counting every photon
Curious about the proportionality
To raindrops on a raindrop day
Knowing seasonality has to be
      Part of the play
But muons keep getting in the way
But this is how I waste the day
But night can't be too far off

I have stumbled upon a scientific thought
That every leaf from every tree
Cannot be as many as every wave
      Ever seen, or unseen
And that every star that there can be
Is not as many as ever been or ever will
But does pollen out number bees
But I'm certain all the deaths outnumber births
Otherwise reincarnation would be a farce
For of all the gods that there have been
How can all but one be a sin

Counting clouds clouds my thoughts
One becomes seven and then is two then one
And then distracted by the occasional dragon
And then should the character wind be included
      In the equation
And what about that child playing down by the river
Long ago I would not have been pestered
But like an ant like Peter chaotically stroll
Without a care of the raven near

I have often like a river
Gladly followed a path whatever
Suffered through however disfigured
Turned right or left whichever inspired
Carelessly sometimes frightfully
Circuitously though arrowly
Never wavering from the goal

(Well, maybe occasionally)
But as the ocean draws near
But and without fear curious that at the end
If not triton at least a putti would be on hand

I tinker with the numbers
Never sure if they slumber
But sure that they wanton in the surf
Sometimes even porny (but not unwelcomed such)
I have no ethics much like statistics
A number is a number whether it is or not
The repellent is not repellent to me
The louche modesty I portray of naughty data virginally
Spotless filth I treasure with a buried pleasure

Every soul a hell does hold
And some more than many
But it is a woe to behold
Not every has a heaven
I crave my heart to see goodness good
For all the good that goodness blesses
Not all the good is goodness

If it weren't for mermaids
The seahorse would despair away
Waves wouldn't want to wave
And tridents would lie in salty shade
If it wasn't for this mystery of the main
The moon would wonder what its worth
To order ebbs or the werewolves return
And forever would the fairies flight
Never grace the night

I am thankful for the mermaid's breasts
Naked throughout the seas
Though rarely but sometimes
Shelled for some special spree with
One of Neptune's nephews or
A nymphous niece but

Never when she comes to me
That's heaven as heaven was meant to be
At least as I suppose, and dream

I believe I've learned how to stop time
Just by ceasing to count
How many calendars converge to a day
But that's the calamity of numbering
But it is more difficult than imagined
-Tremendous thoughts tinkering with thoughts
It is wondrous all the apples on all the trees
And then it leads to pears and then
How many ants have made the trek on how much bark

So many ants but I've been told
There is less then I behold
So a nonterminating number can be rational I suppose
Strange as I understand the finite universe expands
And contains as many stars as there is sand
Infinite in the many lands
As if this universe weren't complex enough
Another is close enough to collide and make it worse
Gödel numbers will have to invade my verse

Sometimes the very air seems filled with
Some things I have never seen
Sometimes in the quiet of the day
I hear faroff music I was not meant to hear
And often times when others are at their praying
And I should be paying sharing my vacant thoughts
I find myself in an empty cove
Rearranging rocks in an orderless display
Until the tide arrives and returns them to their graves

It's difficult to count what
Never was – but not impossible, and
I have found a way to numerate
What has yet but will be
But to quantify what was and now is not

That is what keeps me awake, and yes drunk
The twirling silence in the dark
Attempting to escape my closest watch
Is elementary in comparison

Don't think the baffled snow is baffling
Or that breathing is disturbing
          (Easier if you multiply by two)
Every thread in all the clothes
Every toe and finger - nails too - even
If added together is no matter
Every word of hate even if divided by degree
But love, now this is problematic
Separating love from love that is not love

Stop, the angry unnourished
          Mill mouse has shouted
More times than I have even started
The horse, the hare and even haShem
Beg and plead and threaten
 And while I listen and sometimes agree
The finger moves unwillingly
And it all begins again anew
And the mouse again refuses its jailhouse food

Have you ever heard one word
From the sun bemoaning his going
Just to return, again
The clock rather sings with joy
The ocean roars with laughter
I have never seen an ant along the way
Ever stop to pray
The bee is born an adult ready
To seeming dance in its drudgery

I number all the petals in the world
Fallen, blooming and yet to open
And multiply it by all the thoughts of every eagle
As they transverse (even if they be adverse)

Once I tried to quantify the dust
But that just seemed too much
Then I tried again and then again
Maybe I should try again because it must be done
Even if impossible

I market my soul to the highest bidder
But no devil seems interested - - - whatever
There's lots of time left to count the seconds
And log them in my scattered ledgers
But should an angel in a red hat
Begin to whisper in my ear it's no secret
I will crane to hear however meaningless
Counting all the vowels and every letter
Even if billions upon billions and billions more

After heaven is there another heaven
After fire has consumed everything without respite
Can another fire repeat its course
After day can another day return
I count one river and I count one star
Just a mountain that only rises so far
It must be better to be a rock beneath
        Other rocks beneath other rock

I am Mr. Gam Jue
A living statue
Living forever today
In yesterday
Happy despite the
Calamity surrounding me
At least I can stare
Frozen however
Enjoying what might never have been
Maybe better affront some lonely crypt
So as not to affront the affrontable kind
Than within traffic or
At a counter eating, but not eating, soup
Moai has a purpose but not this statue
Hotei cannot be further from the fact
Gam Jue has a serenity that disturbs others
For how can a life without a life be worth living
Like a statue

As I sat
An angel came
And rested her head
Upon my lap
I could smell
The wild hyacinth, her breath
As roses sprung
Around her legs
Be afraid she whispered
And be not afraid
And write your name
Upon the water
And upon the land
Then disappeared
Fearless I plunged my arm
To the bottom of the pool
And fearless the dragonfly
Stayed upon the lily
But as my fingers traced
The letters I became afraid
As without guidance
They lettered the name
Not once, but twice
And then again

Nomadic in the ocean nomadic
Like a soul in a sea of soul
Foraging in the water forest
Safeless in the safety of being safe
Whether in the slow wilds of the Artic
Or the artless anger of the Atlantic

Like a falling leaf that never falls
A wind that stands still in the storm
A raindrop caught between heaven and earth
Loveless in the love of being loveless
Whether upon the dangerous concrete streets
Or the empty insanity of sky

Mounting heights of mountainous delights
Like pressed palms trembling higher
Sprouting trees to sprout prayers piercing clouds
Hopeless in the hope of being hopeless
Whether fog leaving leaves like incense rising
Or incestuously dripping lower

Woe that oceans become mountains
And angels fall
That blood so safe
Within the vein
Should spill

Dread that dart
Which easily sails
Which gracefully
Dances through the rose scented air
Strikes suddenly thunderously
The target eventually

Fail me faith
More readily than
Give me hope
I, who patiently waits
Thousands of hours for
A slight glimpse of heaven
Who through seasons
Craves but a glimpse of wind
A cool spray of Infinite Ocean

If truth be told
Your anger is a blessing
To behold, as
Rain comforts
The dry earth
After the suns fruitless reign
As clouds release
The wolf's statued pursuit
Permitting him his sole
Resolute

O blessed ebb
That for rocks
Sad delight relaxes
Without the sight
And dear night

Which brings darkness
After too much light
Dreams have their
Dreads and charms
Their blight

I am better hated
Than loved outright
Carefully adrift
Like a man at sea, asleep:
A man on a raft
Panglossian drifting
With the rosy sun above
        Petals on the lake
Though a dunderhead
A flugelman even
        Anchoritic still

Is that your shadow?
Is that the roses sweet scent?
Magical magic!
Profundity:
Pondering the ponderous
In sight of blindness
Even though I see
Though I am here and you there
I cannot believe

The unlikely wind
Stirs up memories of you
As if you were mine
My gargoyle stance
And with holy loving joy
        Bush without a bird
The rose colored swan
Whispers my words into your ear
I could marry you

Petals from the sun

Light my path with scented glow
As butterflies lead
Sky hovers above
(Some stars are meant to do so)
Clouds clod below
Near the zaftig trees
Closing my eyes next to you,
Time evanescent
Dreaming of roses
Dreaming it is not a dream

Dreaming dreams' dreaming

Let me lick your nipple
Or at least kiss your lips
Let me feel your gentle breath
Or a soft touch upon my cheek
If I cannot hold your hand
Just once allow me to harbor a lost hair
Behind your ear – and my fingers linger there
Let me whisper all my joys
Or give my eyes their sole desire
Visit me, and speak my name
Be in all my thoughts
Be in all my dreams

Have I ever told you how much I love you?
Well maybe I should someday

Above these clouds, like an angel
Stratus, cumulus, cirrus
From there to here to there
In an instant

I have the time and freedom to contemplate this; you
While on the other side lies the snark and pogrom
Et hoc genus omne
My own discomfort measured by the genus of the clouds surface
Shambling across the sky with a boulder hovering above
Nonthreatening but present, pleasant even
With the distaff known to be below though hidden

Have I ever told you how much I love you?
Maybe I should be careful if I ever should

Careless upon the ridge like a goat
Volcanic, sedimentary, crystalline, even oceanic
Cofounder of the confounded
Thrust unwillingly toward the heavens
Until though sprawn upon the ledge
The clouds overtake and create hair upon my head
Asleep or awake I dream of angels in my arms
And my lips upon and about their forms and their face
Just grass and dirt and rock
While the soft rhythmic voices are just echoes
And the naked fairies but bees

Have I ever told you how much I love you?
Ever voiced the words which heaven hears?

In the valley I stir within the fold and far from the heights
River, glacier, strath
A depression to cradle my forbidden thoughts –

Like a point I am defined by what I am not

A monad, Grothendiek prime: Bourbaki!
Welcoming being born to love whatever the wounds
Even as I trudge toward the towering ocean
The metonymic marriage my excuse to wake
Bringing Elysium out of this Africa, rest to the raucus
And despite this simony, your smaragdine smile
Gives me mysterious happiness, your chthonic complexion my meaning

Have I ever told you that I love you?
Maybe I should but I can't for I shouldn't
So I guess you'll just have to guess

When I think you
    Have abandoned me
Like a vineyard grown
    Brown and crusty
        Through winter
Like the evening sky after
    The green light of
        The setting sun
Just when I felt the
    Old door of the
        Lamasery should be
            Closed and locked
When the hive readies itself
    Finally accepting
        Any bee not returned
        Must be lost
The warmth of your finger
    On my lowered shoulder
Brings life to the dead vine
    And the green promise of buds
Like the miracle of dawn
    Bringing youth to the morning mass
        And more honey to the hive

My heart, wrapped in
White tissue, then
Tied with blue ribbon,
Sealed within a green bottle
And placed in a white
Cardboard box, taped shut,
Then nailed hidden in a
Wooden chest
Cemented deep in
The earth, buried directly
Beneath the
Planted oak
Fenced and signed

Don't be a setting sun, a
Whistling train receding in
The distance. Don't be a
Rainbow, don't be New
Years Eve. Don't be "Amen"
Or "Last Call," or
The dial tone. Please, please,
Please, -- don't be "The End" of
A novel or a poems last
Word

I do not pretend reality
　　Just fantasy
I have no illusions of
　　Escaping hell
Even while dreaming heaven
　　　　Chained, I pretend
　　　　Freedom
　　　　Dead, I mimic
　　　　Life
But the horror of never
　　　Holding your hand
The despair of never
　　　Daring your lips
　　　Which dangle dearly close
Is never forgotten

My rugose smile is shamed
　　　By your sockdolager beauty
As a weed beside a flower
　　　As a sinner beside a saint
And though a snake hiding within a tree
　　　　No hiss is exhaled
　　　　To tempt
　　　　No slither is meant
　　　　To trip
Just selfish glances for
　　　Moments satisfactions
Memories gathered for
　　　Later haunting
　　　Into sacred sorrows
For endless nights

　　Simple blades of grass
　　　　Pinked and green
　　With sprinkles of snow
　　　　Lamb white sweet
　　Before the sprouting of morning
　　　　Rainbow glow
　　　　I dream you

Sculptured, hidden
In drizzled fog
With Masonic secrecy
I greet the painted entry
Of night, grateful after
The braggadocio of day,
Carrying ahigh a statute
Of a sainted rose
While hidden in an orgy of tears
From solitude
Is it wrong to enjoy the rain
If the cloud remains detached
Is it evil to wander into church
And remain in the back
Maybe I should never
Enjoy the scent or
Praise the petal
And only avow
The thorn
I cannot allow the wave to crash
And ignore its thunder
If the flower is beautiful
Am I to blame
Can I refrain
Laodician

I do not sneer the trees stare
Nor the snark of the crusty creek
Let the clouds their creepy counsel keep,
Then
Creep along – I mark no malignancy:
It is with dragonflies I consort
And with butterflies that I rest

Like a sudden suddenness
The wind suddenly began to wind
Around around me like a twine
Unwrapping the sleep from my eyes;
With mantle to the floor
And like the widow's son at Zarephath
I am here, again, and awake
The dawn which breaks at dusk
Fills my face with sudden illuminatingly bright shade
Levels all the mountain, washes all the past
Wakens all the sleeping birds for a sudden elliptical charge
The meteor strikes
And splinters the seamless sea
Which eases back to be the same
But never quite the same
Then strikes again

      No need to show me the way to Golgotha
      I know the way
      Let me pull the rock back to the cave
      Let me wrap the mantle this time tighter
           This time thrice

Hippocampus dreams are always erotic
After spending its days clinging to objects
The ebbing and unebbing and all
Dependent on the sea grasses clinging
Interrupted only by the ambushing of a crustacean
But especially by the mermaids passing
Who swims by but disinterested
      (As if she would even notice)
But in his dream their bodies are encrusted
As she rides him through the sky and over deserts

59

I cannot pretend:
Having had you naked
    In a car
    In a lot
    In a hallway
Pleasures me
        Even now
Not having you naked
    By the pool
    By an altar
Displeases me
        Even more
Your breasts exposed
On our walks
During dinner
Beneath the moon
    Is my religion
    And even now it's like
        Being banished
          From heaven

If I could have it all
To do over again
    I think I wouldn't
    I know I'd want to
    I definitely would pass
For all the happiness
        More than all
There is this hell of after
    That I cannot endure
For after heaven
I have learned
        Heavenless is worse

I would let the butterfly, if I could
And even a bee, possibly
Sometimes I think if only the tree
But always always
            Especially in Spring
Always or I would be disappointed
            – devastated –
If the swan wouldn't

Never ever any cloud
None, or at least most
Maybe some maybe   .

I would let the rain, any day
And the wind, most enthusiastically
I would give the mist carte blanche
Even mud would have my sufferance
            Its docility is impressive
But the sorrow the ache
            – lamentation –
If the swan didn't

Clearly too I couldn't resist
Let all the clouds
And all clouds friends

But I couldn't the desert
Nor the ocean nor a mountain
No fish no turtle no elk
But the swan but the swan
            - - whatever the swan desires - -

Seriously the sea
Has serpents hiding in the trees
And bumble bees in its beard
Waiting for the waitress to come near
And then, oh dear, it will be too late
The bumble bee will begin to laugh
And the serpent fall out of the tree
   And onto its knees
    Enjoying the jollity joyously
It must be said for the fairies
   Said it must be said
Clouds are not blue nor red
    But green
And grass with its wondrous hue
But it's true, grass is not apricot
Nor amber but alabaster
   Though you may sometimes think
   It's pink

So seriously the sea
Bobs and bobs in its dumb show
With all its knowledge hidden deep
Surrounded in tattermalion mystery
While the sun without a clue
Shines in pageantry of its perceptivity
Under a willow once I heard
How Jesus and Buddha at a party Mohammed threw
Laughed themselves silly at erudition
Believe what you think but
You are always wrong
You may sing what you sing
But there is no song
I heard a story once but
There were no words
I believe what I believe is true
Despite the flowers grunt
Because it knows I know it's false

Seriously the serious sea
Crumbles under its own bombasity

Belittling the worlds wealth of poverty
Then weeps from its sanctimoniousity
 And the sun sometimes hides in shame
And the serpent climbs down to pray
There is so much to know without knowing
There is so much that glows without glowing
And the grass may be purple despite what fairies see

Temerarious
    The skyfull colors blessly
Variegated
How humble the sun
    Gives praise to the night with psalms
Painted on the sky

My eyes rest upon
    The butterfly on the bush
And her sunset blush

And I see the beauty
    Of the brown worm brown with mud
As I would the rose

I know all must glow
    From bark encrusted birch to
Petals on the lawn

My eyes search the rust
    Of the rivers ruggedness
For stones no one wants

Scold the chilly wind
    Like you would scold a child
With a puff of love

Lovely watery
    Sea urchin or rainbow trout
Shy shrimps shelter miracles

My eyes believe truth
    Embracing its fulsomeness
Thorny godliness

Unbelievable
    Earth adores the grateful storm
Innocuously

In the heaven of the heaven of heaven
You reside
And my love for you is written in
A bottle in a bottle in a bottle
Stored and safely bobs along
Across the oceans secretly

A bee on a bee riding a bee
Waves to me
And what I say is what I say so I don't say
And the smile that I smile is not the smile
That I would smile if I smiled honestly
(My butterfly buzzes happily in a bottle on the sea)

In this hell of hell I dread my descent
Into its' hell
The fire that's on fire I would set on fire
And that I cannot chance
But I know in the end it's better
Than to expose my desire for heaven

It is all true what has been said of me
I would rather sit upon a stoop
And talk with a half deaf mouse
Then read a book
It would endear me if you would believe
All the lies told of me
For heaven just yawns when I am brought up
I would half expect and even direct
You to make up a few yourselves
As I have even myself disguised or not
For no truth about me would entertain even a louse

I'm me although I am no longer me
At sea although I no longer a sailor be
Long nights have destroyed the rest of days
An abandoned hermitage with a dark oratory
And ruined sacristy undignified with vestments
Purple or otherwise
Alive with its ineluctable deterioration
For abides the me that is no longer me

I no longer care to see what I cannot see
Nor spelunk among the waves in ecstasy
No word of the reliquary hidden within my shirt
Speak how I hovel with the worst
A rake bearing member of the jacquerie
Reciting perverse verse as litany
None better at hiking up a nun's skirt
No battery of self inflicted flattery
Shall my lips parse but bear the farce

I ask one thing as pure as a bells ring
That afterwards and cleansed of the curse
Keep unsmiled the smile that tempts you in the pew
Like a butterfly avoiding alligators

Satan scares me
But I am not afraid
We have already met
And I admit
He has smeared the paint
Of my existence
But quite frankly
I have done worse to me

Mermaid doesn't scare me
But certainly I am frightened
As ugly always is of beauty
However forgiving is divinity
Sin still skulks from sun
Crows have no place with swans
Just so disgrace is self displaced
Despite the blindness of rain

God does not scare me
Nor am I frightened
I have met many
And each unenlightened
From the arrogance of Jesus
To the false humility of Buddha
        Dare not even mention Jehovah
No belief is best belief
None better than unbelief

I am though scared of nothing
And that deathly frightens me
The emptiness encompassing accusingly
Not of death which lingers like a friend
But of all the rest
The reality and spirituality neither which exists
For all the all that day beholds it's
Curious that nothingness is indigenous to existence

In such a soft spot of light
I must move the paper as I write
To enjoy the words as they are printed
Words from my heart though like
A fiery pointed arrow to pierce my heart
Into submission
Let the ocean ebb I say in silence
Let it ebb farther and to the edge
Until the sea gulls are forced to dry land
And the albatross no longer can force the ship
Into submission
But with the moon so close with all the memories
Of fingers and lips upon my body and breasts
Pressed against my blindness and words whispered towards the west
Who could resist the flow and stem desire
Into submission
Only fate can control the sails, only weather
Can predict itself, so as the stars shine history
Which is extinguished

If the flower could be a tree
It would die from misery
If a bee could suddenly become a butterfly
    Fulfill its dream
It would immediately begin to scream
If rain the breeze and breeze the rain
Mountains rivers and rivers seas
Imagine if the moon became the sun, it would find
The guerdon isn't one

Clouds deform but stay a cloud
Cheerily though without control
No willow would want to be an owl
    For they know
Every heaven returns a hell
River beds whether wet or dry
Stay river beds with dreams of birds of prey:
However empyreal the dream
Its' heaven is a hellish being

There is no sense in knowing
When ignoring is less afflicting

The harrowing of the heart avoided
When it is left fallow

Artificial flowers never wither
Like kissing lips which learn to bicker

Rivers and lakes lie dry in drought
Polar Bears and bees must hesitate

The beauty of the islands shiver
When inevitable hurricanes deliver

There is no sense in craving lips
And yet I crave them like a heaven

Maybe before the morning
       When the moonbeams are in bloom
Maybe after evening when the
       Earth seems empyreal
Away from the banausic day
       With its wooden claims
But into the cloud of trees
       Aspersing magic mizzle
Maybe into your arms to be
       Blessed with naked lips
Or into the tree of clouds with
       Its vagaries of dress
To caress you from afar
       With my witness
My dreams my only mithidate
       For reality
Where my love is privately preserved
       In my phylactery

It is always alarming that the moon
Could allure my thoughts
Away from gloom to you
It's frightening that the flowers
In bloom or even towards doom
Somehow fulfill what nights hopes fear

Often the moon can be a mirage
Flowers fiction and
Adored daydreams daymares
Certainly it can seem at
Times as these that what
Can't possibly must be

Rivers rarely are not riveting
Sometimes even mesmerizing
And take me from myself to you
Even deserts can entice the desperate
With hidden bones beneath the cactus
Like a butterfly slowly from oasis to oasis

Jungles dangle snakes and daylight
Which bar my way through city streets
Sometimes failing but usually successfully
But not in the middle of the garden
I often stand to witness
Everything that can't be seen elsewhere

Vulnerary silence in a wicked world of words
Sometimes shies away from me with its remedy
So only dreams of you can ensure that I endure
And though I sink and sink towards weariness
It's your heaven I am happily entranced with

True
In my evening prayers I thank the Lord
My morning prayers were left ignored
And even truer
My morning prayers ask forgiveness
For evening prayers blindness
My wants are wanting
My lacunae have lacunas
My mermaid dreams are but mermaids
Of seas beyond my seas
And I must drink what I must drink
And leave magic potions for magical beings
But still
When morning passes or
Evenings stomped off to the hills
I become fay with elves and goblins
And play among the leaves

Don't bother staring at me
There is nothing to see
You could play in the ocean daringly
But I am just a trickling stream
Fishless and barely known below the leaves

The heavens are full of stars
And I am but a tiny rock within the giant belt
Passing insignificantly
Even Pluto's never noticed me
Nor any asteroid has glanced this way

A period within a novel
Even Flaubert would not puzzle
A single note accidentally placed
By Beethoven's racing hand mistakenly
Erased except for blindness blame

Drop me a quarter without a word
Glance the other way without blame or shame
Pretend that I do not share the path
I am not worth grumbles or rancor, and remember
Jesus and Buddha did not really mean what they said

I am not the
> Fickle moon
Who wans then
> Looms
I am not the
> Capricious ocean
Shilly-shallying
> About the shore
Not even the
> Monstrous mountain
Which eventually
> Will flitter away
I am your
> Ardent heart
Alive awake or
> asleep

I have been to heaven
And stayed for quite a time
I listened to the music
While eating most delicious bread
The wine was too divine ·
Each glass more sacred than the last
As vast a place as I have ever seen
(Though no vaster than a cloud)
Often I would walk about
Peering into windows as I am want to do
While most preferred to travel now
As angles do
Always there were congregations
In the square in the park
With meaningful conversations
For me to sit and watch
It seemed everyone was there
Not one person was spared
And dogs and cats and elephants
      Doves and vultures bathing in the fountain
Popes and Lamas playing cricket on the lawn
Prostitutes with philosophers with saints
      Vicious sinners with idiots
All were adored and adored
I was finally convinced to live
Eternally in eternal bliss
But then I was asked to leave

Sitting under a rough lemon tree
Catawampus to the sea
Writing flummadiddle poetry
Slantidicular to the world
      Slantidicular to me
Happily to have absquatulated
The queue of humanity
Fearing syzygy or even tmesis
And the foofaraw of its egoosity
Bumptious in any degree
Preferring to loneily apricate
Beside a distant Baobab tree
      Simplely

I wish your heart
        Was beating next to mine
I wish our breaths
        Were intermingling
If your fingers are feeling lonely
My fingers are feeling friendly
Our hairs should be entangled whispers
        Of spells eternally

Why do I have two arms
When I should have four
Why are my toes mumbling
Asking why aren't there more
My pants dream desires of a dress
        To share the floor
My belly wishes for your back
As much as it does your belly
If only your me was with my me
        For my me to adore

It's not that I desire what I desire
Nor even to reach the speed of light though I try
The lips I pray to kiss if present I wouldn't kiss
I fish without a hook and though
I pride myself a bowman I've no arrows in my quiver
I could be the fastest draw but no matter
I would never pull the trigger even if it were loaded with bullets
Let the moon rise and slip away
I'm happy just to be upon the shore
I gladly pray and fast and flagellate
Without promise or even aspiration of transcendence
Let the sun rise and unrise
I neither am joyed or unjoyed
My means are not toward an end
No matter how thirsty I have no need of quenching
The lips I pray to kiss if present I wouldn't kiss

Dare I see your eyes
Dare I touch your hair
Dare I remove your dress and
Gently hang it in the vestiary
My lips pretend to part
Your lips like a sea
For all the loneliness to escape
My ears pretend to hear
Your whispers in the wind
Blushing burning bushes
My thoughts pretend to think
The thoughts you think of me
Paper is my prison while
This bottles but a mirage
And the ocean which it bobs along
Is my mermaids cherished home
So lost at sea is what I long to be
What I desiderate
I adore the day which
Leads to the delights of night
And cherish the prize your body hides
And enjoy what isn't hidden
And detest that dreams are but dreams
And heaven is not my heaven

You would think you could
But it is true
You can't believe a thing
The sun would say
It would like you to surmise
Since the sunrise is such
A sensual delight that
Nothing it has to promulgate
Could be a lie
That its' view, its' blaze of
Breath, is what the what is
In its promontory across the sky
Blabbering that it has nothing to hide
Purring about and spluttering
All the shadows
Opening wide its lips in broadcast
Advertising its angularity and
Adversity to adversity
But night is night despite
The clouds
Night becomes more night
Embracing clouds
And clouds its Gnostic writings
None but night can understand
And so with nothing to hide
It hides
So no one understands

I have painted over
The canvas of me
So you can't see
Me, but rather a pleasant
Scenery out the window
With a bowl of fruit
And flowers on the table
Maybe an accidental spider
As a hint to what perfidy
Lays beneath
The purple and pink petals
On the sink
The strength I have is weakness
This pretty picture punctuates
The irony inspiring
Sarcastically

I have a mermaid
Swimming about my hair
And sometimes she slips down
To lounge in my beard
Sometimes she comes close
       But not near
To my lips but I'm not sure
Since I'm asleep anyhow

I have a seahorse on my shoulder
And another on the other
Both tell me I shouldn't wonder
But accept the mermaids blunder
One tells me to lean close
       The other to lean near
For she sings with magic lips
And has a magical kiss

I have a mermaid
Swimming in my hair
Who occasionally passes by my ear
And the song that I hear
Entrances all my fears
       To not feel fear
And my lips swim to her lips
Until my sleep strikes shore

Could you be as wicked
As I would you be
Walk naked upon the beach
Exposed to the noticing moon
Dance with me
With a blouse so sheer
Revealing what I'm pleased revealed
For all to see including me
Would you allow me liberty
To gently caress
Beneath your dress
An entrance
While we sit upon a couch
In a vestibule
Or if in a hot tub of a lodge as
I would slowly untie your top
Would you smile a lot
Beg me not to stop
Could I kiss your breasts
Could my dream be not a dream
Could this reality I live in
Be the reality I pretend
Could we together
Tickle your nipples
And tenderly engage
Until you behest the rest
Could I be allowed to sit aside
For the pleasure of my eyes
To attend to your body
As you go from there to here
And back and then again
And if I am distracted by a book
You would continue enjoying
Others looks
Or would you banish me
From Atlantis and silence
Your siren singing
And my breathing

I am predestined not to enter heaven
As I am predestined to lose my tribal land
A destiny not quite manifest to me
But not all can be a tree when there is
      Such a need for weeds
Personally in privacy I perceive war is what I should abhor
But I must abide the tide and
Accept what must and cannot but other be
The stolen lands of Palestine
Like California and Texas
Must be stolen since they were stolen
And so we must accept its righteousness
      (Proven by the Rio Grande)
Just as the plague was preordained
All that is will be not otherwise

I don't know why
      I had to starve to death that night
All alone and in the cold
Although I could hear the sated moans
      Of those having too much food
But just knowing that I had fulfilled
Some prewritten decree
I suffered what I must because it was just
Even though the mite I dropped into
The priests' locked slotted box might
Have bought me another clump of
Though moldy bread
But that was not to be and that is fine
      - Who am I to question the divine
How else could you explain
The holocaust and its world-wide pain
Except that it was meant to be
And no human shame could prevent its being
Or slavery or human trafficking

Yes
I am predestined not to enter heaven
Self-exiled actually
As indeed I guess could not but other been

I went out walking yesterday into the forest
With my good friend, the willow tree
We do not stray too far from the stream
Where he loves to spend his days pondering

He knows the sounds and names of all the birds
And asides all our conversations when heard
And sometimes we will stop and chat with Mr. Birch
Who is not particularly happy when we do most times

We follow along an easy path which we made
Which really followed an earlier path some bears had lain
It follows along the stream for quite a ways
Then loops up and around a small hill for an hour or so

We talk of many things (when he's not whistling)
He tells me of the songs he's sung to accompany
The many swallows which always seem to be near
And which entertains the deer which graze close beside him ordinarily

But yesterday quite seriously he was whispering
I had a dream I could barely hear him say
Of a mermaid in a tango with a seahorse
And it worries me what it means

I could never be what I must be he continued
Desperately staring at me and shaking frightfully
For I have had to learn to be what I am not
For so long that I had forgot my other being

I listened with the squirrels and owls quietly
All leaves had ceased to drop and the wind
Without a sound crept close to hear his sounds

What is it asked an ant which was perched upon his arm
Yes asked the bee beside the butterfly for
We all love what you are and you have been a home for us
And I have trusted you with my honey and my family

I'm confused said the bear, we have everything here
And you have always gratefully offered your bark for my backs ease
And just yesterday I saw you looking over the shoulder of some city fellow
Who lay at your feet and read when he was not asleep

The willow tree then shook his head and said
I have said less than I have said and looked at me
Let us return to where I belong he smiled
For I have much to wile about with the stream

Be sure to come tomorrow the tree begged of me
And we will walk the other way and see
If we can say things differently
And so I promised and with a happy wave we parted

But that was yesterday but today
I have not seen the willow tree for hours
And the stream refuses to answer me and I
Noticed the bee who refuses to even look my way
          Being friendly with another tree

I would rather live deepest in the valley
Than atop the toppest mountain
An albatross soaring above the sea whistling melancholically
I could be a bee if I had a hive all to me

A butterfly balanced on a shortish flower
A coolish sun crouched behind a cloud
Sometimes you can see a bird flying in the rain
Or not see an underground stream wandering aimlessly
        Those could be me

It's not that I purposefully live unhappily
It's just it pleases me to be unhappy
Not like a claustrophobic tree spelunking
But like a star reflecting in a turbulent sea

When day has found its way to dawn
And nights finally fallen asleep
When the ocean breeze has ceased its song
And waves their dance unwound
I lay still within my trance
Under the mermaid moon

After all the leaves have fallen
And all the snow has snowed
A different spring arises from the spring
A mist hides tomorrow from tomorrow
Taming me from temptation
Under the mermaid smile

No sailor sails away with sway
Having been belayed entreated
Taunted by the trancing song
To forget all that's been long forgotten
Allured and quivering they yearn to be
Under the mermaid moon

Undines whirl within my dreams
Whisking my skirt of reality
Inveigling finagling and in the end outbraving
Promising osculating ocean waves heart breaking
As I lay spelled besides the sea
Under the mermaid mystery

Toying with a fishbone comb left in the sand
Aphrodite and Venus swimming through the land of my thoughts
Amphitrite and Tethys playing about my hair
Ran playing peek a boo with my eyes
I toy with the fishbone comb left in the sand
Under the mermaid moon

Marvelous in marvelous mystery
A miracle miraculously
I be what I be while she is more than she
Mermaid under the mermaid moon
Lounging and singing while the ocean swoons
Ferociously her gentleness eclipses me

Is that another grave, there,
Waiting for me to sheepishly shamble into?
Another eternity, there, as the opal clouds
Plod past, pummeling me with mere lithe dreams
            The shapes of impossibilities
Drenching my thirst with muddy memories
Yet another grave after so many
And night after night of bearing
The torments of the roots of the living
            Their clawing and stalking
Making even dull sleep prickly
And for what? Another Resurrection?
Another ghostly existence within the garden
Tending the flower which may not be adorned
Whose thorns may never grace my flesh
            Nor share a raindrop of my blood?
I refuse the grave which inches towards me;
Allow me to sit forever still upon the bench
Beside the rose, a silent admirer of petals;
Allow me the pleasure of residing inches from heavens lips
                  Beside her leaves with half feared hopes of accidental
touches
            After an accidental breeze
Shallow is still too deep and harbinges of the sudden depthless doom
Allow me to fill you with winter's snow
Allow me to tend and trim your edges
Within the shadow of the Empress's smile
Let me have this empty life of waiting for
            Intermittent sunshine which may pass by
Give me one winter of woeful hope
            Wild with the knowing senselessness
Take not these feet, these legs, these arms, these eyes

The light has suspired
The light long lived in this such dark place of haven
Suspired and expired
And now I have death to live for
The darker the better
Its felicity of wretchedness
A warmer berth than the coldness of sea
The cloud long suspended in pendulous declaration
Has teared itself away
And now allow the blare of thousands of suns
To scorch my dreary sky
Even taunt me with the dreary happiness of
The mirage of final emptiness
The grave long dug in grateful expectations
Patient and impatient
And now I athirst for its languorous delight
Apathetic of its covetousness
Let me lay in its bed and cover me with the cold warmth to
Enjoy the cinema of colorless nightmares

The worrisome wind
       Worries not for me
And though the skittish sun
       Is skittish for some
It's certainly not skittish for me

The placid lake may be plagued
       By memories and dreams
And fairies fair fairly well
       In the fair night
The forest frets for the
       Forgotten stream
Which languor's beneath its
       Abandoned leaves

I'll carry the lamp
       For the lightening bugs
Who have lost their way
I'll hear the smiles from
       Her daedal eyes
Fantasma more real than visions

It may seem like wandering
The lost stare standing
Frightfully like a
       Barren fruit tree
Rooted whose rare movements
       Are really but the racing wind

The promising river with
       Rumorous imperium
Is simply a share of the rain
       And suffrage for the ocean
Wandering like a wind through earth

I have been stopped by beauty
A single rose standing out in the garden
And not lonely I but other butterflies
Have become mesmerized and fantasize
The danseuse performed with sun and wind
Attitudinizing the beauty of dusk and dawn
While I, shyly incandescent, fluttered
           With a fluttering heart

I have been stopped by beauty
A ripple among ripples upon the silver stream
And a leaf I struggle for ever more against time
To enjoy once more while avoiding the shore
And with other intoxicated leaves devise
Mechanical plans to thwart the sun and wind
To return to the only heaven experienced
           With a destitute heart

I have, I say, been stopped by beauty
A cloud singled out of all the clouds
And though a grain of sand I still imagine
The cloud is there to give shelter just for me
Before I am jostled and buried beneath sand
My kisses and prayers thwarted by the kisses and prayers
From infinite grains of sand
           With an unknown heart

"All the truth in the world adds up to one big lie" - Bob Dylan

I hear the freight train whistle
Entering from the afar
Like a leaf hurtling through space
Above the rumbling trunk
And me lying awake from dreams
Entering from the edge of midnight
Like a log upon the stalled river
Below nights tree full of stars
Nobody knows and that's
The lie which is the truth
Belief takes faith but
Disbelief takes reason
Science may be the whole cloth
Or possibly just a layer
Hold my hand I feel your touch
Whether your hand is held or not
Truth is a wave open to perception
Reality an accident accepted
A forest can be a forest with the trees
But a tree is a tree and must be
Clouds pass and clouds arrive
But once rain the cloud is disdained
Find the flutter in a butterfly
And you will find the butterfly disappears
The lake releases and becomes a river
But come the ocean the river ceases
As birth creates a God and Heaven
But come death the river ceases
And I shall seek the maiden in any form
But exit the maiden and I again am forlorn
I see the flag raised in the morning
And all day wave in all directions
But come the night and it is folded uniform
Don't be misguided by the fairies and sprites
They'll answer all your questions but may not be right
Listen rather to the wind off the ocean
It speaks in mysteries which may never be unraveled

At least though you'll know the truth however indecipherable
Just like the whistle from the freight train powering through the night
I listen to the music without comprehending
Its incomprehensible message
I cannot find among all the pillows a
Pillow worth laying my head upon so
I must accept that my pillow must
Not be a pillow at all
But I have fairies tugging me along and
Since I am not strong I follow their song
Hopefully they have been telling the truth all along
I do not believe and I do not disbelieve
And that's the truth which is a lie
Planets are just planets or
Places for forgotten angels to abide
This monastery is but a monastery and not a monastery
A place to till for gardens delight
And cells for night times rending of light

One angel was there beside me before I met you
(Thank you Raphael)
Then you loved me; now,
All the angels have begun to appear
To congratulate me
Some with stardust still on
Their eyelids, some with smiles
Masking their hardships
--- but I, the lost, have become
Their hope for I have bound the blue flower
--- I have seen the green light
(Thank you Raphael)
I haven't always known but
I have trusted even in my distrust
And you are the final passus
Through all the sunsets
I have been waiting for;
The periscope of my life, my pinghua

How can a Sherman Oaks guy
Fall in love with a San Fernando gal
Can a 15 year old single malt Oban
Be served besides a can of Pabst
It's like a bunch of gangsters playing polo
Dare champagne wake up in a beer mug
Dare an oleander court a gallant rose
Can a convict convince a nun to love
A bête noire an ingénue
A duck a worm

All more possible than a poor monk
partial to a princess

The heartless sun rises
  Destroying dew
The mean birds begin to sing
  With songs that are real
And without care for the bear
  The flower joyously wakens to
Dew destroying dawn and the fawn

A foggy smile is all that remains
  Praying for rain
Grumpy groundhogs poke and bob
  Then scamper and dodge
Stars which whispered wondrous words
  Now are gone and robins ask
Were they ever where they don't belong

Shuffling and shuddering sunlight
  Seeps into all the holes for secrets
Like a thief sneaking about a house
  Pretending to be a shadow
Its sparkling slime floating about
  Creeping about for its own delight
Careless what its crimes destroy

And then it dares to stare amused
  At dusk as it begins to draw
Knowing all the damage it did create
  Cannot be fixed by night and its witches
And soon it will return to continue
  Its destiny as dew destroyer
Until all dreams are forever extinguished

I enjoy to sit
        With coffee and a pen
A book sitting to the side
        To open now and then
And watch the women
        Wander
Past my river bank

All the trees about me
        Never leave me
(At least I pretend)
        Such magical suspense
All of them are lovers
        Though most ignore me
Some glare but maybe one will
        Fake a smile without shaking her head

I neglect
        The crucifix
And ponder
        Who'll come next
Lavishly or
        Scantily
While waves wander to my toes

I enjoy sitting below
        The evening sky magnificently aglow
A book sat to the side
        To open now and then
And watch for women
        Who will suddenly appear
Then disappear

I swear while I was soaring
Through the air around about
Not really anywhere I saw
A cloud not so small that appeared
Suddenly shaped as you
I swirled around amiss with bliss
Not sure but tempted to test and
Once again upon its face your face
I paused in contemplation
Desiring what my lust desired
Until it was impossible to
Persist resist
And with a careless kiss
You turned to mist

Some listen to the ramblings of some dead monk
And think what is said in delirium is atheistic
The irreligious never wandered in sacrilegious
And so unholy strut sanctimonious

Butterflies once flew as worms
Bees trapped in honey combs abused
Flowers scratched the coffins before they bloomed
Half the moon is in delight while half in gloom

Often in the turbulence is peacefulness
Often stench can be traced to a flower
Fallen angels may not be fallen forever
As rain falls but then is risen

Poverty is not robbery of dignity
Sinfulness is not attestation of sinfulness
Hatefulness does not pall saintliness
And dead monks sometimes are not dead

I have a dead friend
    I have never met
With whom I walk about with
    And sometimes address

She is friendly and
    I hold her hand
We walk along the train tracks
    Then back upon the sand

    At times while walking along the shore
She will hold back the ocean
    So I might find a shell
Long buried beneath the waves

I swear sometimes she nudges me
    To see something she adored
Sometimes the silence is witness
    That she is truly present

The foggy night with its foggy moon
    Daring my undared caress
Until the morning mist drapes her nakedness
    And the lips of my unkissed kiss

I confess sometimes she disappears
    Maybe to visit a friend she was want to visit
Sometimes her wished for whispers
    Awaken me to her presence

Reflections are all I have
    Of whom I have never seen
Passing windows of stores
    I have never been

Holding cemetery flowers
    Close to her breast
Her hair both immaculately puffed
    And pressed immensely wet

I find the dead make
    The best friends
Especially those whom
    I have never met

    And maybe when we both are dead
She will hold my hand

Even in the desert I discuss with mermaids
Heaven
And even though she knows my callow
Heart
She forgives my old body
She wears about her neck not a
Crucifix
But an emblem of the tyrant Neptune
Made of walrus bone
  - Its' penis I suspect
But we agree on what is said
Though not the who who said it
And we smile but don't embrace
And although I am obsessed with her
 Breasts
She pretends not to notice
          Despite my propitious perspiration

Saint Mermaid as I am want to call
Her
Wooed in whispers
Swims away in the waves of my mirage
And I below the cactus sleep with parsimonious
Sleep

Simon Bolivar
  Apples in the labyrinth
Farther than the far

At a cool river
  A fisherman's clairvoyance
Lingers as the mist

Like torrential rain
  My tentacular morals
Under orange trees

Like silver powder
  And phantasmagorical
Sunlight and my soul

Hallucinating
  Shoulder to shoulder with dark
Meritorious

Insurmountable
  The dire defeat of winning
And the smell of pears

Perpetual flight
  Sinking into the quicksands
Illegitimate

Degeneracy
  And responsibility
Conciliation

Sometimes I am tricked to wonder if instead of torrents
Noah was commanded to promise a cloudless sky
And God became as a beloved saint ministering to the worthless
A Buddha who smiles on all

What if God stood beside the Abraham with open arms
And as a family hugged the children warm
Without demands but with charm and allowed
All the farms to grow and all to be musical

Moses and Ramses would walk always as family
Miriam and Hatshepsut sisters hand in hand
Without the distraction of deceit or dubiety
Jew and Egyptian as Muslim and Christian

What if, like you or me, he would not have planted such a tree
And allowed the earth to grow in harmony and no births with deformity
And he just sat for all to see in glory and as he professes to be
None would care but to glorify and free of doubt to believe

Jonah and James would have had a simple adventure
With no shame or blindness because of their blunder
If all could be revealed as to Paul
Yahweh indeed would be more like Claus

There is no is nor was nor will be
No sea nor ocean nor lake nor duck
Winter which is not Winter struck
And Spring, that Spring, forever lost, never was

Sun or moon a chance of glance
Could be moon or sun in a flash
Worms may not be worms but birds
And I, well, I am but what

This body made of water is but dust
Old youth wanders like a crippled dove
After trees which reigned by storms uprooted
New flowers bloom the color of rust

A butterfly is but a butterfly
One in a field of butterflies
One field in a field of fields
And I, well I, am but what

Storms are not storms but simply storms
Love is not love but merely love
Faith in reality is faith misplaced
Just as wind which erases Autumn may not

Whence when there is not
Toward what is not
Even here is not a here here
And I, well I, am not even what

When my father was a child
I took him to the park
To swing on the swing set
In the middle of winter
It hadn't started to snow yet
But it certainly was cold
We pretended they were lakes
As we slid across the puddles
And if one of them would break
We were lost forever

It was winter though and
The swings were frozen so
Your pants would stick and rip
If you were so bold so
The baby would cry the whole time
And he would cry the whole way home
Because I would tease him so
But I swear I thought he'd laugh but
Because of the hole in his pants
We were lost forever

It's not easy but
            It must be done
God should be forgiven
            For his sins
                        As well as his sons

We must not harbor hatred
            For all the pestilence
We should not hold a grudge
            No matter all the evil
                        He and his sort allowed

He won't apologize
            His arrogance disallows it
But we must be better than him
            Our Christian Charity
                        With Buddhist Sincerity

Nevertheless it must be done
            With Messianic aura and
Chimeric blessings
            Despite the extreme of perfidy
                        His untamed intelligence allowed to be

Our African Magic purifying
            The pestilential stink of
The calamitous evangelical rites
            We suffered with suffering
                        In nights of night

It must be done
            For heaven without him
Just seems wrong
            And we must do what he does not
                        Forgive all and all means all

A mountain blocks my view of the ocean
As leaves costume the path, deceiving me
The heat causes summer all through autumn
So that winter wakes without warning

Though tis true
      Lit among the trees
           The clouds of fireflies
      My moral torments

The perfidy of the shepherds' crozier
Is not seen in processions of solemnity
But like a bee blown bewilderingly
I'm not really lost though I seem to be
--- Engines move by blowing steam

Though tis true
      Daily the days hear
           Pagan ravings of prayer
      The viaticum

The scent of Jasmine in the hair
And the lingering taste of orange on the ear
Breasts painted by the oceans spray
And the inconceivable sang froid displayed

Though tis true
      My calcined soul
           Resides uncomfortably
      In Castle Magdelena

No truth can ever be found in Truth
Perception immediately changes destination
Hatred of heaven is love's haven
As oceans block the view of mountains

I have a lie I need confess
I have professed and not in jest
To a floccinaucinihilipilification of love
But no truth in that however canorous

Some esteem the Little Witham
Without apprehension of significance
Ruleless rules directionless
Seems to be my quest

A putative lover with amorous desires
With sartorial demeanor believing wickedness is saintliness
Surrounded with an aura of mythological mathematics
Venus and Saturn perpetually aligned

Desperation sometimes desperately
Clings to desperate things
Like a family of trees to possibility
Like a cloud to a limb of sky

But not me: I would fall without a parachute
Then hope for hopeless things
But, of course, while dreading to be concussed
Or worse

Que je croie that is not hoped
 And love that is not and faith
Rain that splatters on my face still runs
Into filthy storm drains

110

I don't know why the elephant is in my dream but there he is
With me in the elevator but he refuses to recognize me
I am in tattered clothes while the beggars' wearing a tux
And why are all the people passing me saying good luck

Her lips come close to me but then they speed away
While I give a scowl to the boxer hiding in the shadow of the truck
I stand there in the crowd naked while the beggar chokes back a laugh
And why are the people saying shame on you when I am innocent

Too many clouds just confuse the sky making flying confusing
While down below I can see all the people playing in the snow
The beggar counts his money while my pockets are sewn
I'd like to scold him but I don't know why

If the elephant steps on my foot how am I going to ask him to move
When he won't even look at me but just stares at the wall
I could go ask the beggar for help but he's smelling the roses in the park
An angel asked me for directions but I wondered why she smirked

I crave to save the saint from the spiders on the wall
While the broken kitchen light keeps staring at me thinking I should take a fall in the next round
I'm feeling faint from hunger while the beggars dining on a table full of food
Oh god I cry why can't I just wake up

If
You could upon some deepest coral
Sit and talk with a mermaid
It would be difficult to hear her wisdom
As her hair wanders with the willow sea
Your thoughts wonder could it fankle you
Besides, her beauty confuses all her canorous words
So that all you hear is her callipyian tail aswirl

If you could sit beside her
No hurricane of heaven could be blamed
For your mesmerized state
She bears the estate of purity and grace
And foolish you to think you have a place
In the palace of her presence

But if you could but if you dared
No more of life would you care
But forever sit upon the coral stairs
Desiring a mermaids momentary glance
Or a sweeping brush of her hair

If you ever have a chance to sit in audience
Carefully resist cacoëthes contact
Just enjoy the moments that she spared
And treasure what treasure treasures
      Treasure what no treasure can compare
And maybe when she swims off like an angel's flight
And in the sea aswirl
A single strand of her hair will still remain
      To be a relic for your altar